MYSTERY STATES SERIES

NORTHEAST REGION

Grades 4–5

D1406380

Project Managers
Thad H. McLaurin and Jennifer Munnerlyn

Writers
Jan Brennan and Mary Sanford

Art Coordinator
Barry Slate

Artists
Nolan Galloway, Mary Lester, Greg D. Rieves, Barry Slate

Cover Artist
Clevell Harris

www.themailbox.com

©2001 by THE EDUCATION CENTER, INC.
All rights reserved.
ISBN #1-56234-448-X

Manufactured in the United States

10 9 8 7 6 5 4 3 2 1

Table of Contents

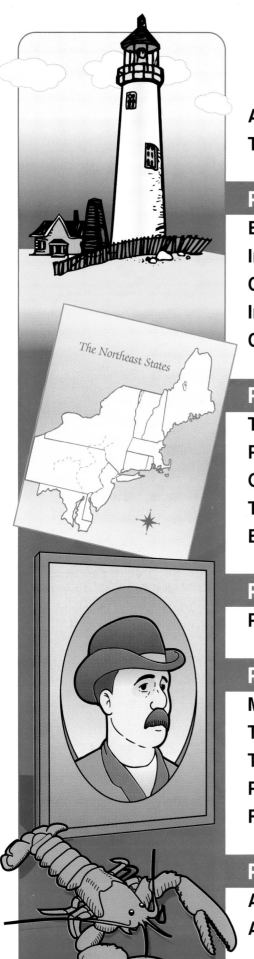

About This Book

Welcome to the Mystery States Series

Through active participation and investigation, the Mystery States series challenges your students to work collaboratively while learning about each of the five U.S. regions. This five-book series supplements and enhances your curriculum and provides a fun, creative, engaging way to teach your students about the U.S. regions. Each book contains a complete social studies investigation of a different region: Northeast, Southeast, Middle West, Southwest, West. Students work in cooperative groups gathering facts and information to form an investigation file to use in identifying a mystery state within each book's region. For ease of use, each book is divided into the following six sections:

- **Teacher's Guide**—Teachers are given detailed, step-by-step instructions on how to use and implement each part of the book.

- **Part 1: Discovering the Mystery State**—Students are introduced, through an original read-aloud, to a family living in the specified region. Using clues embedded in the story and provided clue cards, students work in groups to build an investigation file and identify the state in which the family lives—the mystery state.

- **Part 2: Investigating the Mystery State & Beyond**—Students investigate and research the identified mystery state by completing individual and small-group projects which involve students in a variety of social studies skills. Students also begin to learn more about other states within the region.

- **Part 3: Individual Regional Projects**—Each section contains 20 independent regional projects. These projects are designed to meet the needs of the various learning styles of students. This section also includes a contract for students to complete regarding the plans and completion dates of the selected projects. Also included is an assessment rubric for the teacher to use in evaluating the completed projects.

- **Part 4: Maps & Resources**—Each section contains related state, regional, and U.S. maps; patterns; and resource lists for literature, reference books, web sites, and other contacts.

- **Part 5: Answer Keys & Checklist**—Each section contains a detailed answer key as well as a reproducible checklist that a teacher can use to keep track of each activity completed by each student.

Benefits of the Mystery States Series:
- Supports national social studies standards developed by the National Council for the Social Studies (NCSS)
- Supplements and enhances fourth- and fifth-grade social studies curricula
- Contains a step-by-step teacher's guide
- Encourages active involvement through independent and small-group activities
- Requires higher-order thinking skills and targets different learning styles
- Promotes students' success

Part 1: Discovering the Mystery State

Part 1 is designed to be completed in the step-by-step order presented below. In this section, students are introduced to a family living in a mystery state within the northeast region through a read-aloud story. Students work in small groups to uncover clues embedded in the story as well as complete other activities in which they work in collaborative groups researching, interpreting, and analyzing information to help them predict the mystery state's identity.

Step 1: Have 11 different students, in turn, locate one of these states on a U.S. wall map: Maryland, Delaware, Pennsylvania, New Jersey, New York, Connecticut, Massachusetts, Rhode Island, Vermont, New Hampshire, and Maine. Inform your students that they've just identified the states of the Northeast region.

Step 2: Divide students into six groups. Give each group a copy of "Becca's Dilemma" (pages 8–14). Also, give each student one copy of "Investigation File" (page 15), "Investigation State Checklist" (page 17), the regional and U. S. maps (pages 39 and 40), and a file folder. (Have students keep all reproducibles and gathered research in the file folder throughout the investigation.) Instruct the students in each group to label each Northeast state on their regional maps (page 39). Then direct the students to use a red crayon or colored pencil to shade in the Northeast region on their U.S. maps (page 40).

Step 3: Tell students that they are about to become super sleuths in an investigation of the Northeast region. Explain that you're going to read aloud a story about a family who lives in a state within the Northeast region. Direct students to listen carefully as you read the story. Next, tell your students that you're going to read the story a second time, but this time each student is to jot down on the "Notes" section of her "Investigation File" (page 15) any clues that the story reveals about the state in which the family lives. Remind students to listen for clues, such as geographic references, climate/weather information, and references to occupations, food, plants, and/or animals.

Step 4: After reading the story, allow time for students to compare notes within their groups. Then have a representative from each group read aloud the clues her group discovered. Encourage each group to add to its notes any clues not listed. Have each group evaluate the revised clues and then list in the "Possibilities/Leads" section of page 15 any states in which they think Becca's family might live.

Step 5: Make a copy of page 16; then cut the reproducible into six separate clue cards. Distribute one clue card to each group and inform the group it has several clues to research that will help bring the class closer to the mystery state's identity. Provide ample time for each group to research its clues. Make available a variety of regional references as well as almanacs, encyclopedias, and atlases. (For a list of resources, see page 42.)

Step 6: Hold a conference with each group once it has answered its clues. If the answers are incorrect, guide the group toward finding the correct answers.

Step 7: Have a member of each group read aloud her group's clues and answers. Instruct each student to record each group's clues and answers on the back of her "Investigation File" for future reference.

Step 8: Have each group use the "Investigation State Checklist" (page 17) to check off any states that could possibly be Becca's home based on the gathered clues and clue card information. Then have each group read aloud the states it checked as the other groups record the information in the appropriate columns on their checklists.

Step 9: Instruct each group to use the checklist to eliminate any states not considered as the mystery state and record those states at the bottom of page 15. Then have the group use the checklist information to help it predict the mystery state's identity. After coming to a consensus, have each group member write her prediction on the back of the checklist.

Step 10: Give each student one copy of "Crack the Code" (page 18). Have the student find out the mystery state's identity by completing the reproducible as directed. Take a poll to see how many groups made correct predictions.

Part 2: Investigating the Mystery State & Beyond

The five activities in this section are designed to be completed in any order. Also, the activities are independent of one another so you can select the activities that best fit your students' needs. Each activity can be completed individually, in pairs, or in small groups.

The "Maine" Facts (Pages 20–22)
(Research, Writing)

By completing this activity, students will become more familiar with the mystery state—Maine. Students are challenged to research topics related to Maine, such as location, land features, natural resources, climate and weather, Native Americans, and more.

Materials for each student or group of students: 1 copy each of pages 20, 21, and 22; access to references on Maine and the Northeast region

Directions: Make available various resources on Maine and the Northeast region (see resource list on page 42). After students research the various topics and take notes, have them write complete sentences about each topic in the appropriate sections of pages 20, 21, and 22. If desired, gather the completed work and staple each set of reproducibles along the top, creating a flip booklet. Post each booklet on a bulletin board titled "The 'Maine' Facts." Enlarge, cut out, and color the Maine symbols on page 41 and post them around the display. As an extension activity, have students work in pairs or small groups to research the ten other Northeast states, using the same topics as listed on pages 20 through 22. This will provide excellent information students can use to compare the 11 Northeast states.

Portland or Bust! (Pages 23–24)
(Planning a Trip, Mapmaking, Research, Math)

This activity has students planning a day trip from Bangor, Maine, to Portland, Maine.

Materials for each student or group of students: 1 copy each of pages 23, 24, and 38; road map of Maine; pencil; crayons or markers; file folder

Directions: In advance, make a copy of page 23; then program the "Trip Guidelines" section of the reproducible with the desired cash, gas mileage, and gas price amounts. Next, make a class set (or desired number of copies) of the programed copy. To begin the activity, read aloud the information in the upper left-hand corner of page 23; then read aloud the trip guidelines and directions. Direct students to complete the mileage, cash, and time journals (page 24) as well as the map of Maine (page 38) as directed on page 23. Have students or groups display their completed projects in a file folder as shown. Then direct the students or groups to title the front of their folders "Portland or Bust!" and decorate them.

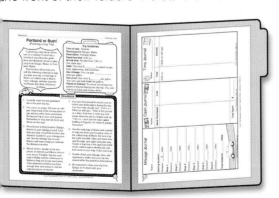

Guess Who (Pages 25–27)
(Researching a Notable Person, Writing)

This activity will allow students to research notable persons from Maine, such as actors, writers, and scientists.

Materials for each student or group of students: 1 copy of page 25; 1 enlarged illustration from page 26 or 27; glue

Directions: In advance, make two or three enlarged copies of each illustration on pages 26 and 27. (Enlargements should be no bigger than 8 1/2" x 11".) Next, assign each student or group of students one of the notable persons from page 26 and 27. Supply each student or group with the materials listed. Then direct students to complete page 25 by using encyclopedias and various other reference materials. Inform students not to use the person's name anywhere on the front of page 25. Once students complete page 25, have them glue the enlarged illustration upside down on the back. Display students' work on a bulletin board titled "Who's Who Gallery." Tack one 9" x 12" sheet of construction paper on the board for each student or group. Then mount each "Guess Who" page to one of the mounted sheets of construction paper by stapling only along the top of the reproducible. Encourage students to visit the board, read a "Guess Who" page, guess the identity of the notable person, and then flip up the sheet to reveal the answer.

The Lobster Company (Pages 28–30)
(Writing a Business Proposal, Research, Simulation)

In this activity, students will research the lobster industry of Maine, then plan and write a business proposal for a new lobster company.

Materials for each student or group of students: 1 copy each of pages 28, 29, and 30

Directions:

Step 1: Have each student or group research the lobster industry by completing page 28; then have them use this information to complete the graphic organizer on page 29. Inform students that they will have to complete a business proposal form from the bank in order to get a loan to open the lobster company. Explain that page 29 is an organizer in which they can plan out their requirements for the company before actually completing the business proposal.

Step 2: After students have completed page 29, have them use the organizer to help write the business proposal (page 30). To complete the simulation, each proposal must be submitted to the banker (you). Read over the proposal and accept or decline the proposal based on the information or lack of information provided in the business proposal. If the proposal is declined, have the student or group rework the proposal and submit it a second time.

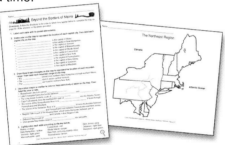

Beyond the Borders of Maine (Pages 31–32)
(Mapmaking, Research)

This mapmaking activity takes students beyond the borders of Maine to learn more about the ten other states in the Northeast region.

Materials for each student or group of students: 1 copy of page 31, 1 enlarged copy of page 32 on an 11" x 14" sheet of paper; crayons or colored pencils

Directions: Provide each student or group of students with the materials listed. Also make available various reference materials on the Northeast region (see resource list on page 42). Instruct each student or group of students to complete pages 31 and 32 as directed. If desired, place an enlarged outline map of the Northeast region (see map on page 39) labeled with the appropriate state names in the center of a bulletin board. Arrange the student-created maps around the enlarged map. Title the display "Beyond the Borders of Maine."

Part 3: Individual Regional Projects

The research topics, contracts, and rubric in this section are designed to provide each student with an opportunity to successfully complete research on the Northeast region. The projects are grouped into four quadrants according to different learning styles.

Pick-a-Project (Pages 34–36)
(Research)

Materials for each student: 1 copy each of pages 34, 35, and 36; access to a various reference materials on the Northeast region; a variety of art supplies

Directions:

Step 1: Assign each student (or allow them to choose) one or more projects from one or more quadrants on page 34.

Step 2: Provide each student with a copy of the "Pick-a-Project Contract" (page 35). After discussing due dates and other pertinent information, direct each student to complete the contract(s) and sign at the bottom. After reviewing each student's contract, add your signature at the bottom.

Step 3: Provide each student with a copy of the "Pick-a-Project Rubric" (page 36). Discuss the grading criteria on the rubric with your students. After a student completes each assigned project, use the rubric to evaluate her project. (Page 36 can be used to evaluate up to four projects per student.) Using the rubric will help you evaluate each student's project(s) on eight different criteria, using a scale of 1 to 5 (1 = Poor, 3 = Good, 5 = Outstanding).

Part 4: Maps & Resources

Part 4 contains related state, regional, and U.S. maps; symbols; and resource lists for related literature and reference books, Web sites, and other contacts. Many of the maps and resources are used in conjunction with the activities in Part 1 and Part 2.

- Maine Outline Map (page 38)
- The Northeast States (page 39)
- The United States (page 40)
- Symbols of Maine (page 41)
- Resource Guide (page 42)

Part 5: Answer Keys & Checklist

Part 5 contains a detailed answer key as well as a reproducible checklist that you can use to keep track of each activity completed by each student.

PART 1: DISCOVERING THE MYSTERY STATE

Becca's Dilemma

"Miss Rebecca Paige Harper, where are you?"

Startled out of her private world of thoughts, Becca looked up to see her dad's scrutinizing look.

"Oh, sorry, Dad. I was just thinking…" Becca said cautiously.

"Well, save your thinking for school tomorrow. Tonight we're celebrating!" Dad announced with enthusiasm as he turned a loving gaze toward his wife sitting across the table.

Becca and her family dined at their favorite restaurant to celebrate Mom's recent important and special sale. She had sold many of her oil paintings before, but now one of them was going to be hanging in the White House! Becca was certainly proud of her mom. She was a very talented artist and deserved this night of celebration. It was just that she had something else on her mind. Becca figured she might as well get it out in the open.

"Dad, I'd like to propose…"

"A toast!" Dad chimed in. "Of course—that's a great idea, honey. Go right ahead," he added as he raised his water glass with a smile.

Becca's eyes made a quick sweep around the table. Her two younger brothers, Doug and Andy, struggled as they both tried to raise their water goblets higher than the other. Mom looked lovingly at Becca, anticipating what she might say. And Dad gazed at her expectantly. Becca fingered her cut glass goblet for a moment, then dramatically began.

"What's the big deal?" She paused just long enough to invoke a beginning sense of shock, then continued. "I'll tell you what the big deal is. We've known for years that Mom's paintings are awesome. But now the whole country—maybe even the entire world— will know who Kate Harper is. Pretty impressive, Mom!" she concluded with a genuine smile.

"Thanks, honey," whispered a misty-eyed Mom.

"Three cheers for Mom," shouted Doug.

Dad added, "You've been waiting a long time for a break like this, Kate. We're all proud of you!"

"Hey, speaking of waiting, when is our food coming?" asked the ever-hungry Andy. "I can't wait for my chowder!"

As if on command, a waiter appeared with a tray laden with steaming seafood, wholesome breads, and crisp, fresh salads. Everyone settled into eating with only an occasional line or two of dialogue. When Becca finished her meal, she looked out at the harbor.

Three cheers for Mom!

She loved it here. There was always something exciting to watch—the constant action of boats loading and unloading, coming and going. There was nothing boring about this place. Becca's thoughts switched back to her earlier attempt at conveying her summer proposal. She had desperately wanted to talk about it. She knew her chances of convincing her parents were decreasing with each passing day. Maybe on the way home, when they would have a good half-hour ride, she could bring it up again. That should be enough time to talk it through.

But once again, Becca was upstaged, this time by Andy, who chose that night of all nights to grapple with the sobering fact that the lobsters he had waved to on the way into the restaurant weren't there just to look at. He had thought that the lobsters in the showcase tank were the restaurant owner's pets. As they were leaving the restaurant, Andy walked past the tank to wave good-bye to his lobster friends, but discovered that one was missing. When Dad simply replied, "He was someone's dinner!" it was more than six-year-old Andy could handle. It took the majority of the ride home to console him. Where he thought lobster meat came from (or chicken for that matter) was beyond Becca. "It's a good thing I like potatoes and beans because that's all we'll be eating for a while," she thought.

It was bedtime before she knew it, and Becca had not had the opportunity to talk to her parents about her summer plans. Just as she started to feel a little panicky, she remembered a homework assignment that she thought might do the trick. Last week she had completed a writing assignment in which she had to convince someone about something. In her paper she had tried to persuade her parents to let her get a kitten. Even though a kitten was out of the question because her dad was allergic to cats, both her parents and her teacher said the paper was very well written and incredibly convincing. So all she had to do now was write another persuasive letter—but this time for real.

After saying good night to everyone and getting ready for bed, Becca closed her bedroom door, put the necessary supplies on her nightstand, turned off the light, and climbed into bed.

With a flashlight in one hand and a pen in the other, she slithered under the covers and prepared herself to write. About a half hour later, she emerged as if from a cocoon, smiling brightly and feeling confident. She folded the letter and tiptoed into her parents' bedroom, where she silently left it on their bed for some interesting late-night reading. She quickly fell asleep, convinced that this letter would do the trick.

Becca awoke to find a letter on her pillow. After rubbing the sleep out of her eyes, she tore the envelope open. She quickly scanned it to find responses like "Sure!" and "Sounds like a great idea!" but decided to read it word for word when those phrases didn't jump out at her.

Dear Becca,

First of all, we'd like to thank you for your honesty. A face-to-face conversation would have been our first choice in dealing with this issue, but we understand how crazy our lives have been lately, and perhaps we wouldn't have had time to talk about it until the summer was long gone! You raised many good points in your letter. You organized your thoughts and presented them in a very mature fashion.

But we are sorry to say that although your three main issues of being bored while at our camp, not liking the "roughing" aspect of camp, and being lonely up there are well taken, we cannot allow you to stay at home for the summer. Yes, Dad will be here during the weekdays, but he will be at work, leaving you basically alone all day long.

Let's all try to think about the situation and see if we can come up with a different solution to the problem. Perhaps if we put our heads together, we can come up with ways to make our summer vacation at the lake one that will be enjoyabl—even exciting—for you this year. We understand your concerns and want you to be happy. Let's think about it today and we'll talk about it at dinner tonight.

Love,
Mom and Dad

Enjoyable? Exciting?! Those were not two words that came to mind when Becca thought about spending the summer at the lake. She *had* already given it plenty of thought and knew there was no other solution.

As Becca showered and dressed for school, she found herself laughing sarcastically at the thought of what suggestions her parents might come up with: Just think of all the books you can read! Your cousins will be coming from Auburn to visit. You can earn extra money by baby-sitting! The boring list would go on and on.

Becca decided to sacrifice breakfast so she wouldn't have to confront her parents and stayed in her room until she heard the bus honk for her. She charged down the stairs, tossed a cool "see ya tonight" in the direction of her parents, and rushed out the door. As she sank into her seat on the bus, she breathed a sigh of relief. At least she wouldn't have to deal with them until that night.

⬤ ⬤ ⬤ ⬤ ⬤ ⬤ ⬤ ⬤ ⬤ ⬤ ⬤ ⬤ ⬤ ⬤

Kate Harper put her brush down with a sigh. It was a spectacular day. The cloudless sky was a dazzling blue, and golden sunbeams danced off the lightly rolling surf. But in spite of these perfect conditions, Kate couldn't keep her mind on her work. Deep in thought, she wandered along the rocky coast. She had an unsettled feeling about her daughter. She knew Becca was disappointed and angry at their refusal, but she also knew their decision was right. A 12-year-old girl is not ready to stay home alone for the majority of the summer days, no matter how mature and responsible she is. Somehow she had to come up with something that would help Becca look at her summer vacation in a new light.

Kate sat down and looked out at the water. Everything that she loved about their summer place—the peaceful mornings and quiet evenings; the lack of modern conveniences; the free time to read, paint, think—all of that was pure boredom and torture for Becca. What would be exciting and action-filled for her? Kate's thoughts were gently nudged back to the present by something that moved slowly and gracefully out on the horizon. "That's it!" she exclaimed passionately as she stared ahead. She rushed back to her easel, packed up her canvas and supplies, and bustled back to her car. She had some phone calls to make, a little research to do, but she was sure she had hit upon Becca's summer saver!

⬤ ⬤ ⬤ ⬤ ⬤ ⬤ ⬤ ⬤ ⬤ ⬤ ⬤ ⬤ ⬤ ⬤

School was uneventful at best for Becca that day. She couldn't recall one thing that she did during her classes. All she could think about was hauling wood for the stove, lugging jugs of water from the spring, sitting for hours reading in total silence—day after boring day.

"Hey, Becca, heads up!" called Coach Giller.

Becca's thoughts were jolted by a soccer ball that was heading right toward her. With a quick lunge to the right, she headed the ball right into the goal.

"Nice shot," Coach said, "but where were you? You looked like you were a million miles away!"

"No, just about 200 miles," Becca said with a laugh. "Sorry, Coach, I'm ready to practice now."

Becca joined her team to practice for the upcoming soccer tournament. Running laps, doing drills, taking shots on goal—Becca loved all of it. She felt alive when she was playing soccer. But, of course, there was no soccer at the lake.

After a great hour of practice, Becca walked home with her two best friends, Sarah and Julie.

"My parents said no to my idea of staying home from the lake this summer," Becca said flatly. "They said we'll talk about it tonight after we've all had time to think about other solutions to the problem."

"Did you come up with anything?" Sarah asked.

"NO!" Becca exclaimed. "I've done all the thinking I can and there's no other solution. There's nobody up there that I can do anything with and there's nothing to do except swat flies."

"I wish I could swat flies with you," Julie said with a giggle. "I have to stay home most of the summer. I can't go to camp this year because Mom and Dad are trying to save money for Meagan's college tuition, so camp is out!"

The three girls walked on in silence. Suddenly, Becca's face lit up.

"Hey, I've got an idea! Maybe you can come to the lake with me for a week or two. Since Dad has to work most of the summer, he comes up for the weekends. Maybe he could bring you up some Friday, leave you with us for a week or two, and then bring you back on a Sunday when he goes home! Do you think your parents would let you go?"

Julie answered first. "Absolutely! They're feeling kind of guilty because I can't go to camp!"

"And I'm not doing much this summer either," Sarah added. "I'm going to soccer camp in August, but July is basically open. I would love to go!"

"Well, let me talk to Mom and Dad tonight. They're generally pretty cool and I have plenty of space in my bedroom at the cottage. I'll call you tonight and let you know!" The girls all said good luck and good-bye and headed home.

● ● ● ● ● ● ● ● ● ● ● ● ● ●

Tom Harper slid into the driver seat of his van. He thought about all the miles he'd be logging in the next few months. He sure wished he could spend the entire summer at the lake with his family, but his job wasn't as portable as Kate's. He needed to be at the furniture factory not only to work at his own trade, but also to oversee the other craftsmen. So weekends in July and three weeks of vacation in August would have to suffice.

Suddenly, Tom's thoughts were jolted from vacation time to the present as he slammed on the brakes for a mother duck that came waddling across the street. She took her time as she led her little brood of fluffy brown ducklings to the pond on the opposite side of the road. Before starting up again, Tom glanced back to make sure his cargo was unharmed by his quick stop. He didn't want Becca's surprise to be broken before she even got a chance to consider it. He had worked through his lunch hour and into the afternoon to make what he thought would be a tool to save Becca from having to "rough it." When all of the ducklings were settled and his cargo was secured, he continued his short journey home, full of anticipation and hope that his daughter would feel more optimistic.

● ● ● ● ● ● ● ● ● ● ● ● ●

The conversation at dinner was somewhat strained and sparse; Doug and Andy talked the most. Becca thought that maybe her parents were annoyed at how she had left so abruptly that morning with barely a good-bye. But right after dinner things brightened. Mom approached the table with a blueberry pie in one hand and a brochure in the other. The broad smile on her face erased Becca's fears. As Mom cut pieces of everyone's favorite pie, Becca scanned through the brochure. It was about sailboats.

"Mom, why do you have this?" Becca asked with an inquisitive little smile.

Mom explained the revelation she had had earlier that day when she was out painting. She thought that having an exciting new sport to concentrate on this summer would ease Becca's boredom. She shared pricing information and suggested that perhaps Becca could pay for part of the sailboat with baby-sitting money.

"What do you think?" Mom asked anxiously.

"Before you answer," Dad interjected, "tell me what you think of this." He jumped up from the table, hustled off to the garage, and returned wheeling a sturdy wooden cart. He parked it right next to Becca and said, "This is your own personal caddie that will help you tote wood for the stove and water from the spring. It should serve you well—just as you do us!"

Becca couldn't believe it. Her parents had really given her problem some very serious consideration and hadn't come up with boring, silly suggestions.

"You guys are the best!" she exclaimed. "I'm sorry I was so rude to you this morning. I just—"

Her mom cut her off. "It's okay, honey. We were young once, too. You woke us up to the fact that the lake is not the perfect place for everyone all the time. You needed a few changes to make it work for you this year. We understand. I'm just glad you were able to tell us about your feelings and needs."

"So," Dad added, "I want to know what you came up with today. It looks like Mom worked out the boring aspect. I worked on the 'roughing' part. Did you work on the loneliness?"

"As a matter of fact, I did!" Becca said with a laugh. "What do you think about bringing Sarah and Julie up with us for a week or two?"

Mr. and Mrs. Harper exchanged glances. "Do you think we can handle the three of you?"

"You two can handle anything. You're the best!"

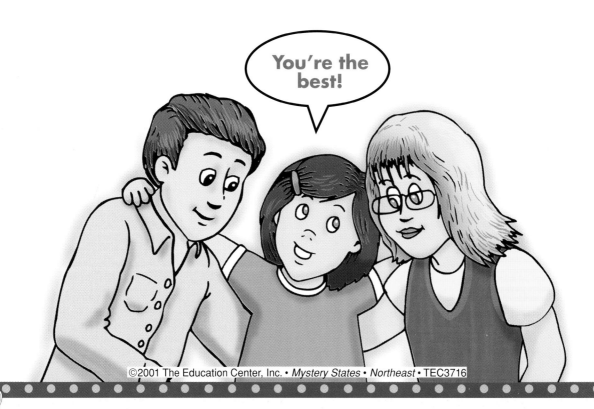

Investigation File

Investigator's Name: _____

Notes

Possibilities/Leads

Eliminations

Clue Cards

CLUE 1

The Appalachian Trail

1. Through which states does this trail pass?
2. Which of these states are coastal states?

©2001 The Education Center, Inc.

CLUE 2

Becca and her family live in the town of Auburn.

1. Which states, entirely east of the Mississippi River, have a town named Auburn?
2. Which of these states are coastal states?

©2001 The Education Center, Inc.

CLUE 3

Becca was named after the main character of *Rebecca of Sunnybrook Farm,* which was written by a distant relative.

1. Who is the author of *Rebecca of Sunnybrook Farm*?
2. Where was the author born?
3. Name several places where the author lived.
4. Where does the book take place?

©2001 The Education Center, Inc.

CLUE 4

Becca's dad is a furniture maker whose business depends greatly on the logging industry.

1. In which two states did the first sawmills appear in the United States? Why?
2. During the 1860s and 1870s, what two states were centers of the lumber industry?
3. Since 1920 what two regions of the United States have been centers of the lumber industry?

©2001 The Education Center, Inc.

CLUE 5

Becca and her family enjoy eating potatoes.

1. Which five states are the leading producers of potatoes?
2. Which of these states are coastal states?
3. Where did white potatoes originate?

©2001 The Education Center, Inc.

CLUE 6

Famous artist Winslow Homer is an inspiration to Becca's mother, Kate.

1. Where was he born?
2. Where did he die?
3. Where did he complete most of his sea paintings?
4. His studio was located in what large city?

©2001 The Education Center, Inc.

Investigation State Checklist

STATES	Group 1	Group 2	Group 3	Group 4	Group 5	Group 6
Connecticut						
Delaware						
Maine						
Maryland						
Massachusetts						
New Hampshire						
New Jersey						
New York						
Pennsylvania						
Rhode Island						
Vermont						

Crack the Code

Directions: To discover the nickname and the name of the mystery state, use the code box below to help you find a letter that matches each shape. Write the corresponding letter in the blank beneath each shape.

Examples: ⌐ = A   ⋀ = Y

Code Box

A	B	C
D	E	F
G	H	I

N	O	P
Q	R	S
T	U	V

J

M   K

L

W

Z   X

Y

PART 2:
INVESTIGATING
THE MYSTERY STATE
& BEYOND

Name(s) _____

20

The "Maine" Facts

State Capital: _____

State Tree: _____

State Flower: _____

State Animal: _____

Physical Land Features

Natural Resources

Climate & Weather

Location

N

E

W

S

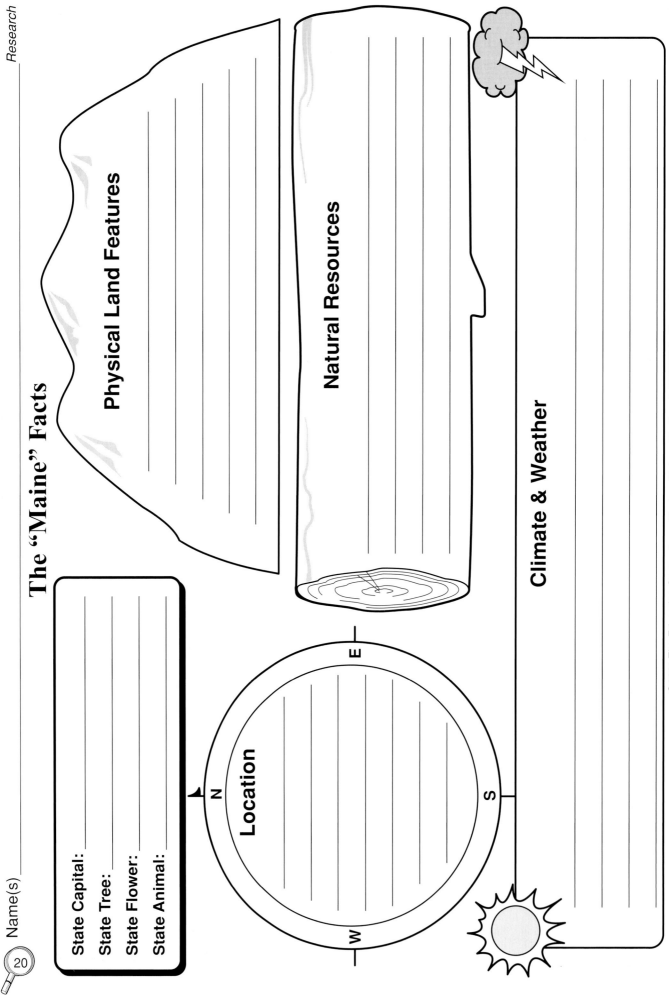

Name(s) ______________________________ *Research*

Native Americans

History

Famous Landmarks

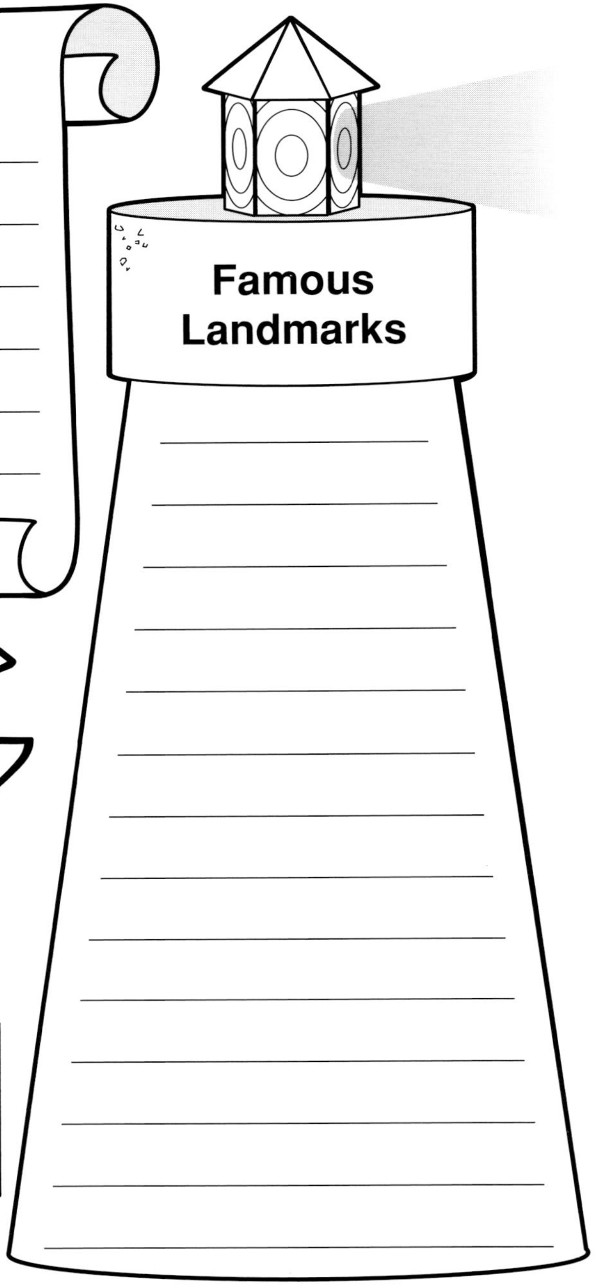

Food

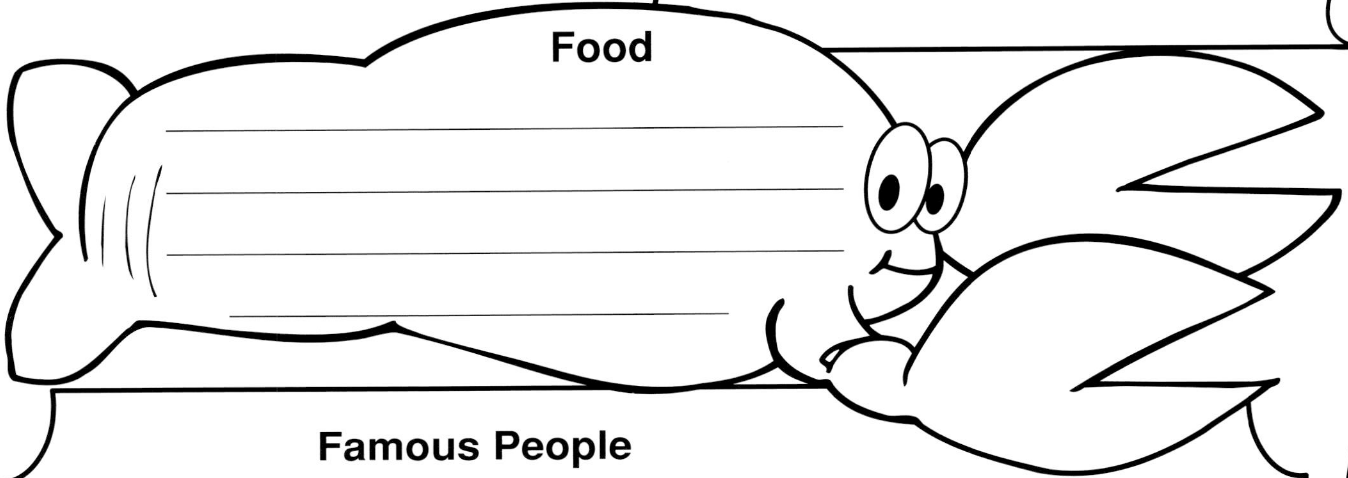

Famous People

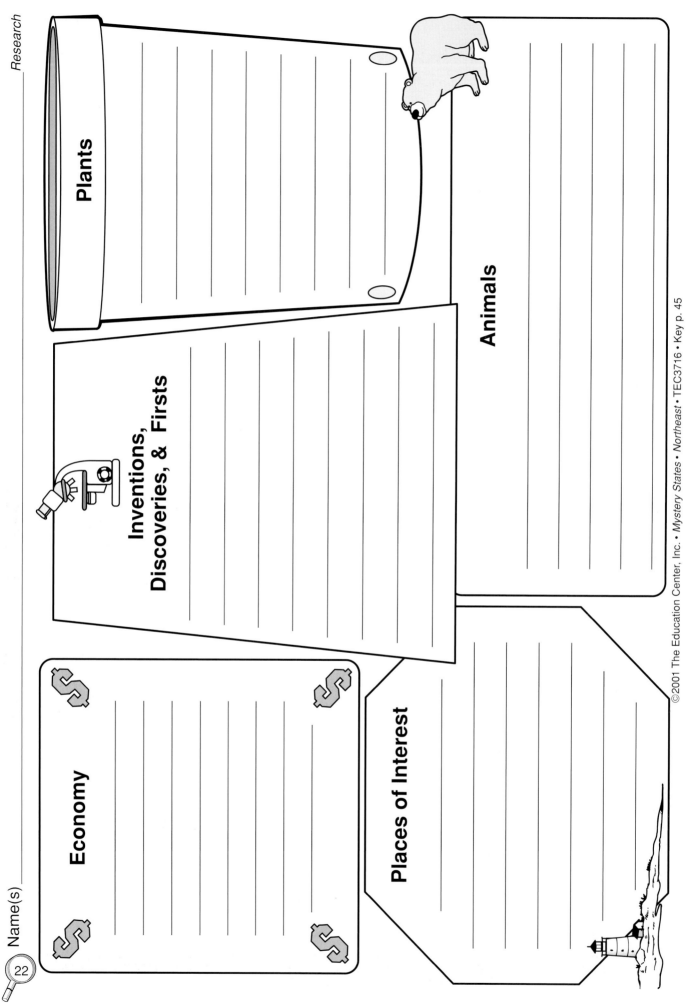

Name(s) _____

22

Plants

Animals

Inventions,
Discoveries, & Firsts

Economy

Places of Interest

©2001 The Education Center, Inc. • *Mystery States • Northeast* • TEC3716 • Key p. 45

Portland or Bust!
(Planning a Day Trip)

Is planning a day trip an adventure or a mystery? It won't be a mystery if you follow the guidelines and directions shown to plan a trip from Bangor, Maine, to Portland, Maine.

Your teacher will provide you with the following materials to help you plan your trip: a road map of Maine; an outline map of Maine; cash, mileage, and time journals; and books and other references on Maine.

Trip Guidelines

Time of year: Summer
Starting point: Bangor, Maine
Destination: Portland, Maine
Departure time: 8:00 A.M.
Arrival time: No later than 7:00 P.M. (the same day)
Cash: You have $_____ to spend on gas, food, sightseeing, and souvenirs.
Gas mileage: Your car gets _____ miles per gallon.
Gas price: Gas costs $_____ per gallon. Your car's gas tank holds ten gallons.
Places of interest: You must visit at least two places of interest during your day trip. (You can visit more if time and money allow.)

Directions

1. Carefully read over the guidelines above for your day trip.

2. Your car is on empty. Fill your car with gas. Keep track of the money spent on gas and any other items purchased during your trip in your cash journal. Remember to stop and eat lunch and dinner on the way!

3. Record your starting location (Bangor, Maine) in your mileage journal. Each time you stop, record the location and distance traveled in your mileage journal. Use the mileage key on your Maine road map to help you estimate the distance traveled.

4. Ahead of time, decide on the two places of interest you'd like to visit on your way to Portland. Use the road map of Maine and the references on Maine to help you locate each place. Then determine whether you have enough time and money to visit the selected places of interest.

5. Use your time journal to record your activities and observations during the day. Your first entry should read, "8:00 A.M.— Filled car with gas." Think of this journal as a diary. Feel free to write any comments about the places visited, such as "1:00 P.M.—Just saw the state capitol building in Augusta. It's made of granite. Awesome!"

6. Use the road map of Maine and a pencil to help you draw your traveling route on the outline map of Maine. Be sure to label roads traveled, cities and towns traveled through, and sights along the way. Create a map key in the space provided on the outline map to identify any symbols used on your map. Color your map.

7. Double-check your mileage, time, and expenses to make sure your trip has stayed within the guidelines listed above.

8. Be prepared to share your trip from Bangor to Portland with your classmates.

Mileage Journal

Name: _____

Starting location: _____

Distance: __0__ miles

Stop 1: _____

Distance: _____ miles

Stop 2: _____

Distance: _____ miles

Stop 3: _____

Distance: _____ miles

Stop 4: _____

Distance: _____ miles

Stop 5: _____

Distance: _____ miles

Stop 6: _____

Distance: _____ miles

Total distance: _____ **miles**

©2001 The Education Center, Inc.

Cash Journal

Name: _____

Items Purchased	Cost
Total Spent	$

©2001 The Education Center, Inc.

Time Journal

Name: _____

Time	Activity
8:00 A.M.	Filled car with gas.

©2001 The Education Center, Inc.

©2001 The Education Center, Inc. • *Mystery States • Northeast* • TEC3716

24

Guess Who

Clue 1: Birthdate

_____

Clue 2: Occupation/profession for which this person is most noted

_____

_____

Clue 3: Information that ties this person to the state of Maine

_____

_____

_____

_____

Clue 4: More specific details about this person and his/her accomplishments

_____

_____

_____

_____

_____

Flip up the bottom of this page to reveal the identity of this mystery Maine person.

25

Who's Who Gallery

Hannibal Hamlin

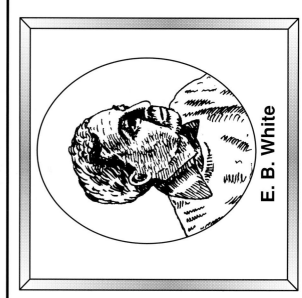

E. B. White

Margaret Chase Smith

Harriet Beecher Stowe

George Bush

Stephen King

Who's Who Gallery

Liv Tyler

Henry Wadsworth Longfellow

Chester Greenwood

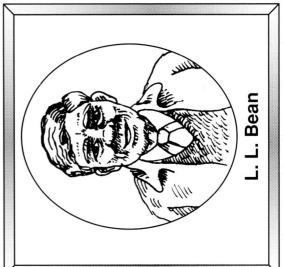

L. L. Bean

Joan Benoit Samuelson

Dorothea Dix

The Lobster Company
Research It!

You and your business partner(s) want to start a lobster company. The bank requires that you present a *business proposal,* which explains the purpose of your business and how you plan to start it. The banker will study your proposal carefully and decide if your new company is a good risk for her to lend you money.

Directions: In order to write your business proposal, you need to become an expert on lobsters and the lobster industry. Research the answers to the following questions to help you become more familiar with lobsters and the lobster industry. Write your findings on the back of this sheet. Check off the appropriate lobster as you complete each question.

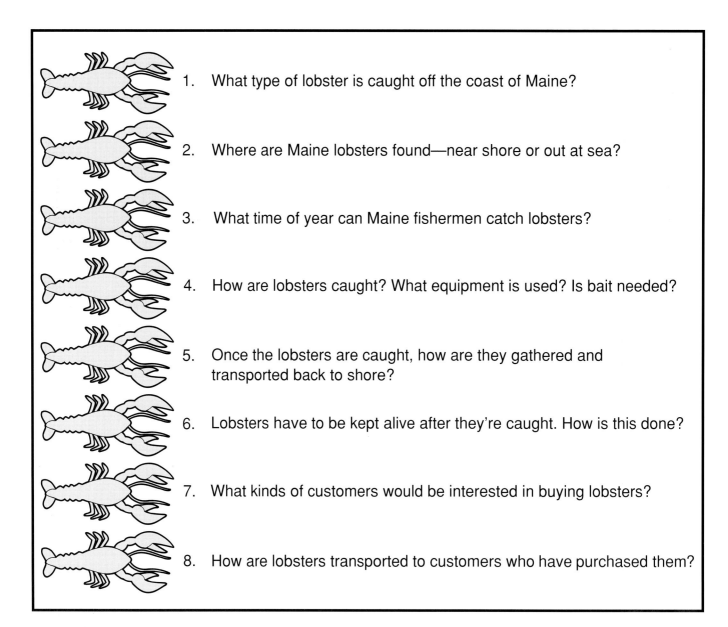

1. What type of lobster is caught off the coast of Maine?

2. Where are Maine lobsters found—near shore or out at sea?

3. What time of year can Maine fishermen catch lobsters?

4. How are lobsters caught? What equipment is used? Is bait needed?

5. Once the lobsters are caught, how are they gathered and transported back to shore?

6. Lobsters have to be kept alive after they're caught. How is this done?

7. What kinds of customers would be interested in buying lobsters?

8. How are lobsters transported to customers who have purchased them?

Name(s) _____

The Lobster Company
Organize It!

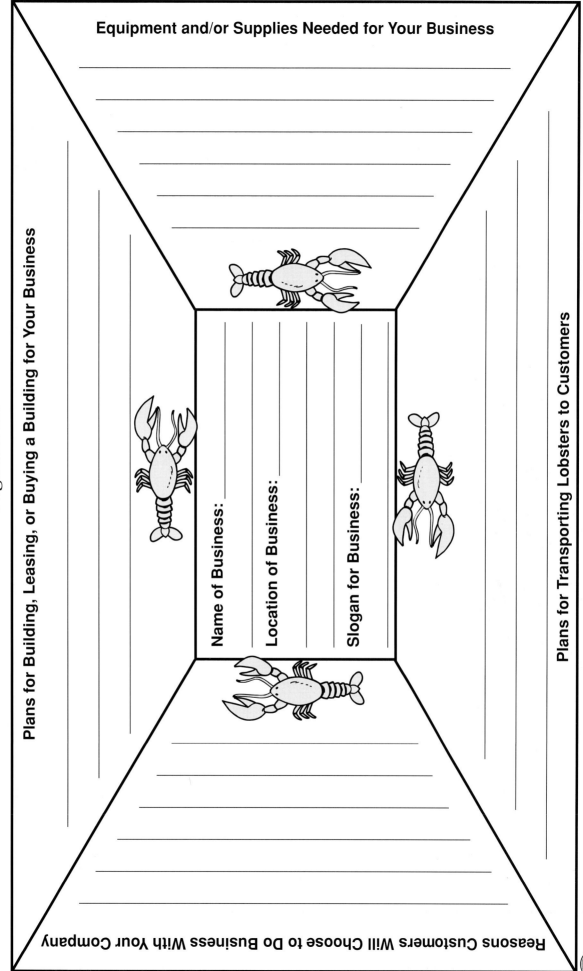

Equipment and/or Supplies Needed for Your Business

Plans for Building, Leasing, or Buying a Building for Your Business

Name of Business: _____

Location of Business: _____

Slogan for Business: _____

Plans for Transporting Lobsters to Customers

Reasons Customers Will Choose to Do Business With Your Company

Fishermen's Bank of Maine
Business Proposal

_____   _____
Name(s) of Applicant(s)   Date

1. Name of proposed business: _____

2. Proposed location of business: _____

    _____

3. Explain why this is a good location for your business. _____

    _____

    _____

4. Do you plan to build, lease, or buy the building(s) in which the business will be located? Why? _____

    _____

5. Equipment and/or supplies to be purchased: _____

    _____

    _____

    _____

    _____

6. Write a brief description of the proposed business. Be sure to include the purpose of your business, who some of its customers may be, and why these customers will prefer to do business with you rather than another company. _____

    _____

    _____

    _____

    _____

    _____

    _____

    _____

    _____

    _____

    _____

7. Does your business have a slogan and/or logo? Yes ☐ No ☐ If yes, provide a sample on the back of this page.

Name _____

 **Beyond the Borders of Maine**

Directions: Follow the directions in the order in which they appear below to complete the map on page 32. Write answers on the blanks provided.

1. **Label each state with its postal abbreviation.**

2. **Draw a star on the map to represent the location of each capital city. Then label each capital city on the map.**
   - _____ is the capital of Maine.
   - _____ is the capital of New Hampshire.
   - _____ is the capital of Vermont.
   - _____ is the capital of Massachusetts.
   - _____ is the capital of Rhode Island.
   - _____ is the capital of Connecticut.
   - _____ is the capital of New York.
   - _____ is the capital of Pennsylvania.
   - _____ is the capital of New Jersey.
   - _____ is the capital of Delaware.
   - _____ is the capital of Maryland.

3. **Draw three brown triangles on the map to represent the location of each mountain range. Then label each mountain range on the map.**
   - The _____ stretch from northern New Hampshire through northern Maine.
   - The _____ stretch across central Vermont.
   - The _____ are found in northern New York.

4. **Use a blue crayon or marker to color or trace each body of water on the map. Then label the river or lake.**
   - Moosehead Lake is in central _____.
   - Lake Champlain forms the border between _____ and _____.
   - The Long Island Sound is south of _____.
   - Cape Cod extends from the southeastern part of _____ into the Atlantic Ocean.
   - The source of the Susquehanna River is in _____. It flows through Pennsylvania and Maryland.
   - The source of the Delaware River is in _____. It forms the borders between _____ and Pennsylvania and between Pennsylvania and New Jersey.
   - Niagara Falls is part of the Niagara River, which forms the border between part of _____ and Canada. Label Niagara Falls.
   - Delaware Bay is east of _____.
   - Chesapeake Bay divides most of _____ into two parts.

5. **Lightly color each state according to the key below.**

Maine—orange	Connecticut—red	New Jersey—gray
New Hampshire—yellow	Rhode Island—purple	Delaware—light blue
Vermont—light green	New York (and Long Island)—blue	Maryland—dark green
Massachusetts—pink	Pennsylvania—brown	

The Northeast Region

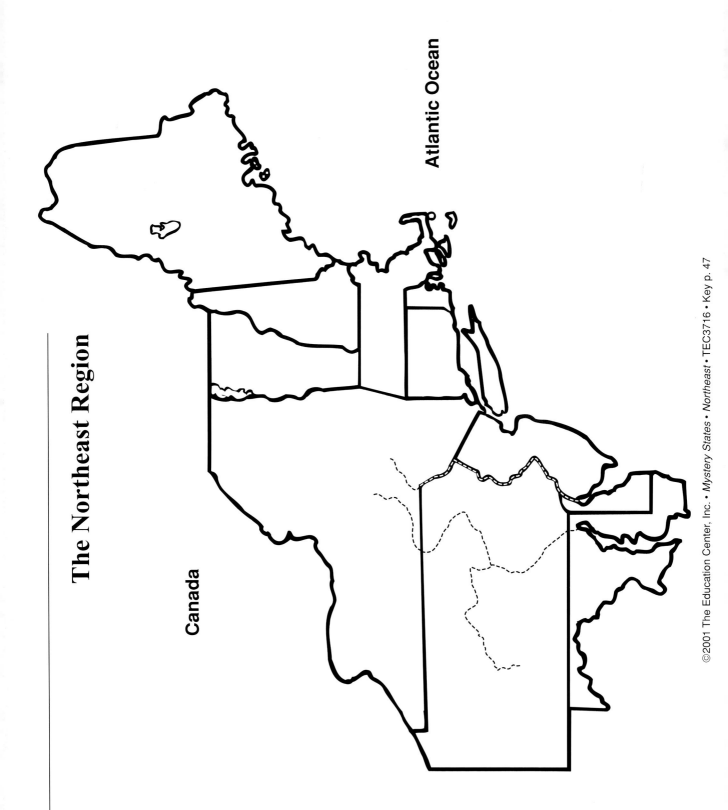

Canada

Atlantic Ocean

PART 3: INDIVIDUAL REGIONAL PROJECTS

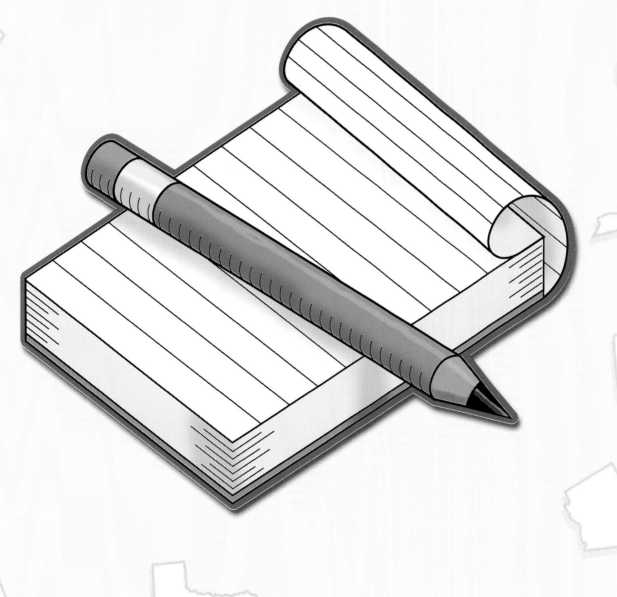

Pick-a-Project

Group 1

- ☐ Compile a scrapbook for a state in the Northeast.

- ☐ Create a cookbook with recipes and foods from states in the Northeast.

- ☐ Make an ABC picture book based on a Northeast state to share with a younger student.

- ☐ Make a newspaper that details current events of a city in the Northeast.

- ☐ Select a state in the Northeast and list the top 30 reasons why it's a great state.

Group 2

- ☐ Write a sequel to Becca's Dilemma.

- ☐ Write a poem or ode about a state in the Northeast.

- ☐ Write three diary entries detailing Becca's summer adventures.

- ☐ Write a letter to the tourism office of a state in the Northeast explaining why you would like to move there.

- ☐ List the advantages and disadvantages of living in the Northeast.

Group 3

- ☐ Write an essay explaining Maine's involvement in the Revolutionary War.

- ☐ Compare and contrast Maine with two other states in the Northeast.

- ☐ Select a state in the Northeast and design a timeline showing the important events in its history.

- ☐ Write a letter to the governor explaining why fishing is important to Maine's economy.

- ☐ Summarize an important event in the Northeast region's history.

Group 4

- ☐ Design a detailed travel brochure for a state in the Northeast.

- ☐ Write and perform a song about the Northeast.

- ☐ Make a 24" x 36" construction paper quilt about the Northeast region.

- ☐ Design a new state seal for Maine or another state in the Northeast.

- ☐ Write and perform a radio or television program about the Northeast.

Pick-a-Project Contract

Name ______________________________

Project ______________________________

Due date ______________________________

Materials/resources needed ______________________________

____

Plan for completing project ______________________________

____

____

____

Student signature ______________ Teacher signature ______________

Pick-a-Project Contract

Name ______________________________

Project ______________________________

Due date ______________________________

Materials/resources needed ______________________________

____

Plan for completing project ______________________________

____

____

____

Student signature ______________ Teacher signature ______________

©2001 The Education Center, Inc. • *Mystery States • Northeast* • TEC3716

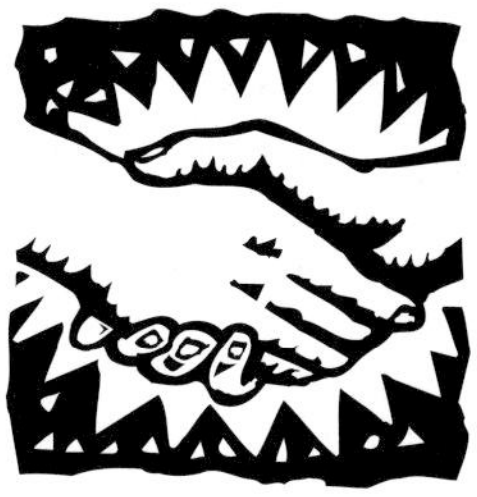

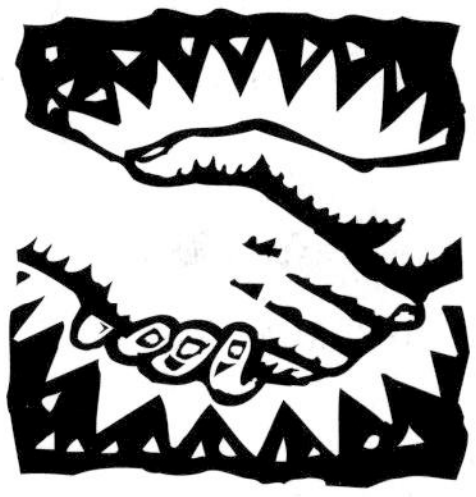

Pick-a-Project Rubric

Name _____	Project _____	Project _____	Project _____	Project _____
The contracted number of projects has been completed.	1 2 3 4 5	1 2 3 4 5	1 2 3 4 5	1 2 3 4 5
Each project has been turned in on time.	1 2 3 4 5	1 2 3 4 5	1 2 3 4 5	1 2 3 4 5
Each project has been completed according to the directions on page 34.	1 2 3 4 5	1 2 3 4 5	1 2 3 4 5	1 2 3 4 5
Each project is neat and pleasant to read.	1 2 3 4 5	1 2 3 4 5	1 2 3 4 5	1 2 3 4 5
Each project is well organized and easy to understand.	1 2 3 4 5	1 2 3 4 5	1 2 3 4 5	1 2 3 4 5
Each project has been proofread for spelling and punctuation, and any errors have been neatly corrected.	1 2 3 4 5	1 2 3 4 5	1 2 3 4 5	1 2 3 4 5
Each project contains accurate information about Maine or the Northeast.	1 2 3 4 5	1 2 3 4 5	1 2 3 4 5	1 2 3 4 5
Each project is creative and fun.	1 2 3 4 5	1 2 3 4 5	1 2 3 4 5	1 2 3 4 5
Final score:				

©2001 The Education Center, Inc. • Mystery States • Northeast • TEC3716

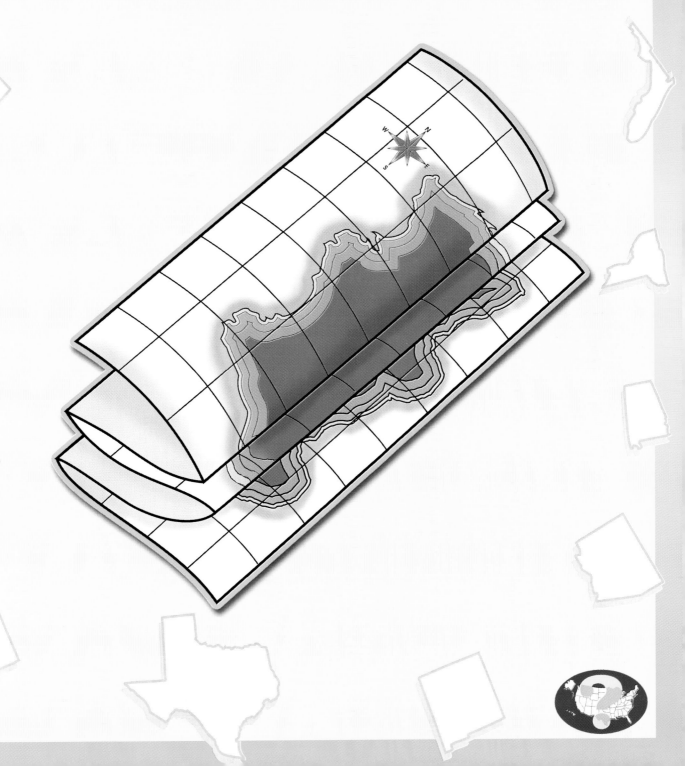

PART 4:
MAPS
& RESOURCES

MAINE

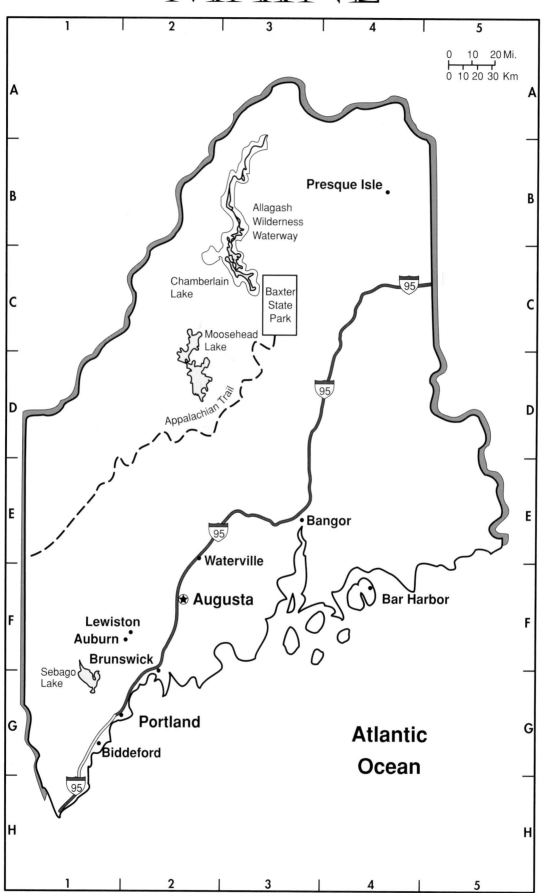

A1 A2 A3 A4 A5

Presque Isle •

Allagash
Wilderness
Waterway

95

Chamberlain
Lake •

Baxter
State
Park

Moosehead
Lake

95

Appalachian Trail

95

• **Bangor**

• Waterville

⍟ **Augusta**

Bar Harbor

Lewiston
Auburn •

Brunswick

Sebago
Lake

Atlantic
Ocean

• **Portland**

•**Biddeford**

95

THE NORTHEAST STATES

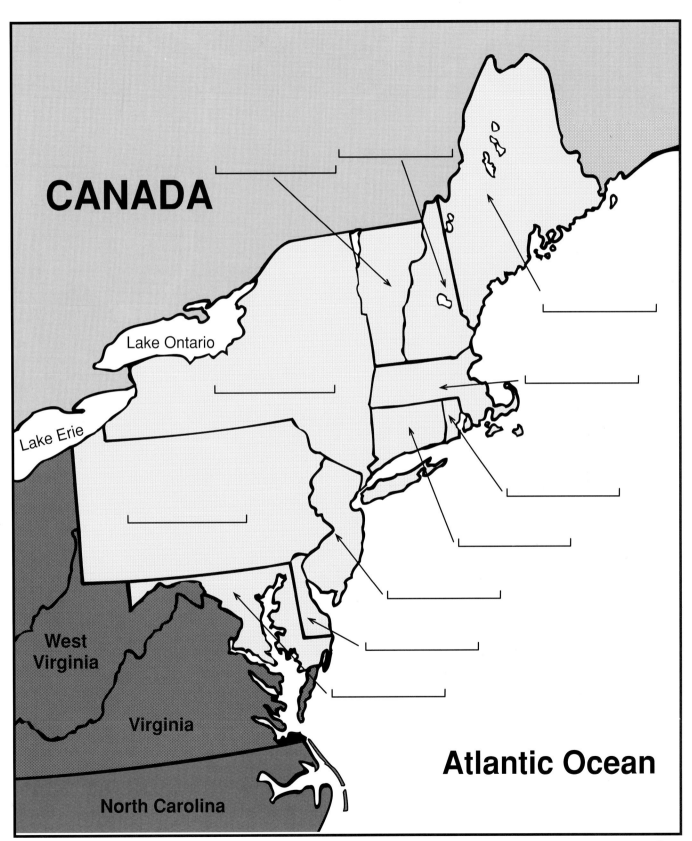

CANADA

Lake Ontario

Lake Erie

West Virginia

Virginia

North Carolina

Atlantic Ocean

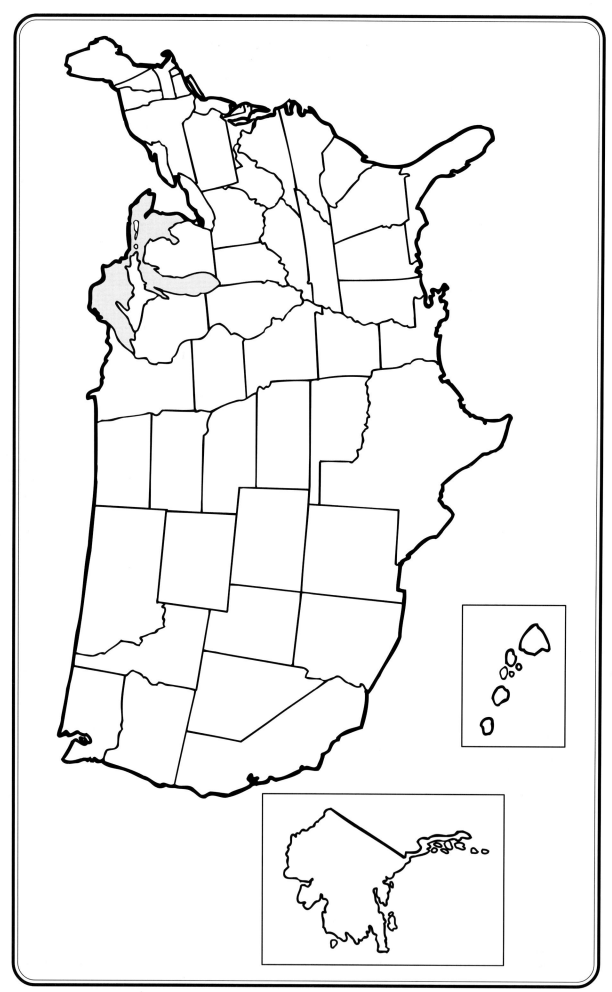

THE UNITED STATES

Symbols of Maine

Resource Guide

Picture Books and Novels

A Beach for the Birds by Bruce McMillan (Houghton Mifflin Company, 1993)
Birdie's Lighthouse by Deborah Hopkinson (Aladdin Paperbacks, 2000)
Blueberries for Sal by Robert McCloskey (Viking Press, 1976)
Burt Dow: Deep-Water Man by Robert McCloskey (Viking Press, 1989)
Fire in the Wind by Betty Levin (Beech Tree Books, 1997)
Going Lobstering by Jerry Pallotta (Charlesbridge Publishing, 1990)
The Island Alphabet: An ABC of Maine Islands by Kelly Paul Briggs (Down East Books, 1995)
Island Bound by Betty Levin (HarperCollins Juvenile Books, 2000)
Island Boy by Barbara Cooney (Viking Press, 1991)
Keep the Lights Burning, Abbie by Peter and Connie Roop (Carolrhoda Books, 1987)
Lost on a Mountain in Maine by Don Fendler (Beech Tree Books, 1992)
One Morning in Maine by Robert McCloskey (Viking Press, 1976)
The Original Freddie Ackerman by Hadley Irwin (Aladdin Paperbacks, 1996)
Patrick's Tree House by Steven Kroll (MacMillan Publishing Company, 1994)
Project Puffin: How We Brought Puffins Back to Egg Rock by Stephen W. Kress (Tilbury House Publishers, 1999)
Rebecca of Sunnybrook Farm by Kate Douglas Wiggin (Tor Books, 1999)
The Sign of the Beaver by Elizabeth George Speare (Yearling Books, 1994)
Time of Wonder by Robert McCloskey (Viking Press, 1989)

Reference Books

Appalachian Trail: A Photographic Tour by Carol M. Highsmith and Ted Landphair (Crescent Books, 1999)
The Coast of Maine Book: A Complete Guide by Rick Ackermann and Kathryn Buxton (Berkshire House Publishers, 1999)
Frommer's Portable Maine Coast by Wayne Curtis (IDG Books Worldwide, 1999)
Maine: An Explorer's Guide by Christina Tree and Elizabeth Roundy (Countryman Press, 1999)
Maine: Off the Beaten Path by Wayne Curtis (Globe Pequot Press, 1998)
Rocks and Minerals (Peterson Field Guides) by Frederick H. Pough (Houghton Mifflin Company, 1998)
Scholastic Atlas of the United States by David Rubel (Scholastic Inc., 2000)
Winslow Homer Watercolors by Helen A. Cooper (Yale University Press, 1987)

Web Sites

(Current as of September 2000)

www.state.me.us/sos/kids/homepage.htm—Maine Secretary of State's Kid's Page
www.state.me.us/sos/kids/links/statelinks.htm—other states kids' pages
www.visitmaine.com—the official Web site of the Maine Office of Tourism
www.maineattraction.com—site with information on attractions in Maine
www.state.me.us/doc/prkslnds/chart.htm—Maine Bureau of Parks and Lands
www.destinationmaine.com/region.shtml—regions of Maine
www.destinationmaine.com/lghthous/lighthse.shtml—Maine's lighthouses
www.mainetourism.com—Maine Tourism Association

Contacts

Maine Office of Tourism
59 State House Station
Augusta, ME 04330
(207) 287-5711

Maine Tourism Association
P.O. Box 2300, 325B Water St.
Hallowell, ME 04347
(207) 623-0363

Acadia National Park Nature Center
P.O. Box 177
Bar Harbor, ME 04609
(207) 288-3338

PART 5:
ANSWER KEYS
& CHECKLIST

Answer Keys

Page 16
Clue 1:
1. Connecticut, Georgia, Maine, Maryland, Massachusetts, New Hampshire, New Jersey, New York, North Carolina, Pennsylvania, Tennessee, Vermont, Virginia, West Virginia,
2. Connecticut, Georgia, Maine, Maryland, Massachusetts, New Hampshire, New Jersey, New York, North Carolina, Virginia

Clue 2:
1. Alabama, Georgia, Illinois, Indiana, Kentucky, Maine, Massachusetts, Michigan, Mississippi, New Hampshire, New York, Pennsylvania, West Virginia
2. Alabama, Georgia, Maine, Massachusetts, Mississippi, New Hampshire, New York

Clue 3:
1. Kate Douglas Wiggin
2. Philadelphia, Pennsylvania
3. Pennsylvania, California, Maine, New York City
4. Maine

Clue 4:
1. Virginia, Maine
2. Pennsylvania, Michigan
3. Pacific Northwest and the South

Clue 5:
1. Idaho, Washington, Maine, Oregon, Wisconsin
2. Washington, Maine, Oregon
3. South America—Bolivia, Chile, and Peru

Clue 6:
1. Boston, Massachusetts
2. Maine
3. Prout's Neck, Maine
4. New York City

Page 18
THE PINE TREE STATE
MAINE

Page 20
State Capital: Augusta
State Tree: White pine
State Flower: White pine cone and tassel
State Animal: Moose
(Answers will vary for the topics below. Possible answers are listed.)
Location:
Maine is the northeasternmost state, bordered by the Atlantic Ocean, Canada, and New Hampshire.
Physical Land Features
Maine is about 320 miles long and 210 miles wide. Total area equals 33,215 square miles. Maine is divided into three natural land regions:
- Coastal Lowlands—southeastern Maine; extends inland 10 to 40 miles from the Atlantic Ocean; lies near sea level; sandy beaches; over 400 offshore islands
- Eastern New England Upland—located northwest of the Coastal Lowlands; 20 to 50 miles wide; in Maine, extends from Canada down to New Hampshire; ranges from near sea level to 2,000 feet above sea level; contains many lakes and swift streams; mountains cut through the center of the region
- White Mountains Region—northwestern Maine; 5 miles wide in the north and 30 miles wide in the south; contains hundreds of lakes and Maine's highest mountains
Natural Resources
Forests cover about 90 percent of Maine (about 18 million acres). Maine has very rich soil and an abundance of minerals, including granite and limestone
Climate & Weather
Maine is cooler than most states. Arctic air and coastal winds keep temperatures cool; 15°F is the average January temperature and 67°F is the average July temperature. Average precipitation is 41 inches and annual snowfall ranges from 70 inches near the coast to 100 inches in the interior. Coastal areas experience a great deal of fog.

Answer Keys

Page 21

Answers will vary. Possible answers include the following:

Native Americans

The Abenaki and Etchemin tribes of the Algonquins lived in what is now Maine before white settlers came to Maine. The Abenaki lived west of the Penobscot River; the Etchemin lived east of the river. Early white settlers of Maine and Native Americans lived in peace.

History

A.D. 1000—Vikings, led by Leif Ericson, most likely visited Maine.

1498—John Cabot, an Italian exploring for England, probably reached Maine.

1524–1604—French explorers, including Samuel de Champlain, explored Maine.

1607—Pioneering English colonists came to Maine, but due to Indian troubles they returned to England.

1620s—The English returned and made many permanent settlements.

1763—The Treaty of Paris put an end to France's claim to Maine.

1775—The first naval battle of the Revolutionary War took place off the Maine coast.

March 15, 1820—Maine became the 23rd state of the United States.

Famous Landmarks

Portland Head Light—one of the oldest and most famous American lighthouses; was built in 1791

Acadia National Park—located in southeastern Maine and the only national park in New England

Wadsworth-Longfellow House—located in Portland; the boyhood home of the famous poet Henry Wadsworth Longfellow; Maine's most popular historic site

Food

Blueberries—the largest blueberry-growing state, raising 98 percent of the low-bush blueberries in the United States

Apples—the most valuable fruit crop

Lobsters—largest annual catch of lobster of any U.S. state

Potatoes—Maine's most valuable farm crop

Famous People

George Bush was the 41st U.S. president and a lifelong summer resident of Maine.

Hannibal Hamlin was vice president to Abraham Lincoln.

Winslow Homer was a famous landscape and marine painter who painted many seascapes at Prout's Neck, in Maine.

Henry Wadsworth Longfellow was a famous poet and author.

Harriet Beecher Stowe wrote *Uncle Tom's Cabin* while living in Brunswick, Maine.

E. B. White was the author of *Charlotte's Web*.

Cindy Blodgett is one of the top women basketball players in the country.

Page 22

Answers will vary. Possible answers include the following:

Economy

The *service industry* (wholesale/retail trade, real estate, finance, insurance) accounts for 75 percent of Maine's gross state product. *Manufacturing* (paper products, clothespins, lobster traps, matches) accounts for 19 percent of the gross state product. *Agriculture* accounts for 2 percent of Maine's gross state product.

Inventions, Discoveries, & Firsts

Earmuffs were invented by 15-year-old Chester Greenwood in 1873.

The first chewing gum sold commercially in America was made by John Curtis, a Maine logger.

Edwin Arlington Robinson, born in Head Tide, Maine, was the first person to win the Pulitzer Prize for poetry.

Plants

Trees found in Maine include: balsam, basswood, beech, hemlock, maple, oak, pine, spruce, and white and yellow birch trees.

Plants found in Maine include: anemone, aster, bittersweet, black-eyed Susan, buttercup, goldenrod, harebell, hepatica, Indian pipe, Lady's-slipper, mayflower, orange and red hawkweed, white oxeye daisy, and wild bergamot.

Animals

Some animals found in Maine include: beavers, black bears, bobcats, foxes, lynxes, martens, minks, moose, raccoons, skunks, squirrels, and white-tailed deer.

Places of Interest

Some tourist attractions in Maine include: lighthouses, Acadia National Park, Wadsworth-Longfellow House, and coastal beaches.

Page 26

George Bush—Bush was born in 1924. He has spent many summers in Kennebunkport, Maine. Bush became the 41st president of the United States in 1989.

Margaret Chase Smith—Smith was born in 1897 in Skowhegan, Maine. In 1948 she became the first woman ever elected to the U.S. Senate.

Hannibal Hamlin—Hannibal was born in 1809 in Paris, Maine. Abraham Lincoln chose him as his vice presidential running mate in the 1860 election.

Stephen King—King was born in Portland, Maine, in 1947. He has written several best-selling novels.

Harriet Beecher Stowe—Stowe was born in 1811. She lived in Brunswick, Maine, during the Civil War period. Stowe wrote *Uncle Tom's Cabin.*

E. B. White—White was born in 1899. He moved to North Brooklin, Maine, and lived there for 28 years. White is the author of *Charlotte's Web, Stuart Little,* and *The Trumpet of the Swan.*

Answer Keys

Chester Greenwood—Greenwood was born in 1858. He lived in Farmington, Maine. Greenwood invented many everyday items, including earmuffs.

Dorothea Dix—Dix was born in 1802 in Hampden, Maine. She developed ways to care for the mentally ill.

Liv Tyler—Tyler was born in 1977 in Portland, Maine. She is an actress.

L. L. Bean—Bean was born in 1873. He lived in Freeport, Maine. He developed a lightweight boot with leather tops and a rubber sole known as the "Bean Boot."

Henry Wadsworth Longfellow—Longfellow was born in 1807 in Portland, Maine. He became a well-known American poet.

Joan Benoit Samuelson—Samuelson was born in Freeport, Maine, in 1958. She became the first woman to win a gold medal in the first ever Olympic® Games women's marathon event.

1. American lobsters, also known as Maine lobsters or True lobsters, are caught off the coast of Maine.
2. Lobsters are found both near shore and out at sea, depending on the season. During the warmer months, some lobsters tend to move closer to the shoreline. In the fall they migrate out to deeper waters.
3. Maine lobster fishermen are allowed to fish year-round. However, most prefer not to fish for lobsters during the rough winter months.
4. Traps called *pots,* which are made of narrow pieces of wood or metal, are used for catching lobsters. The traps are baited with fish and attached to a rope line that lowers the cage to the ocean floor. Each string of pots can contain as many as 50 pots.
5. The traps are usually checked every two to four days.
6. A lobster pound is usually used to store live lobsters. Often a pound is located along a sea water embankment where seawater is pumped into a circulating tank system. Some inland, self-contained tanks are set up similar to a home saltwater aquarium to store the live lobsters.
7. Individuals who enjoy cooking and eating lobsters, supermarkets, and restaurants would be possible customers.
8. Lobsters can be stored in special holding tanks and shipped from Maine to other places around the world.

2. Draw a star on the map to represent the location of each capital city. Then label each capital city on the map.
   - _Augusta_ is the capital of Maine.
   - _Concord_ is the capital of New Hampshire.
   - _Montpelier_ is the capital of Vermont.
   - _Boston_ is the capital of Massachusetts.
   - _Providence_ is the capital of Rhode Island.
   - _Hartford_ is the capital of Connecticut.
   - _Albany_ is the capital of New York.
   - _Harrisburg_ is the capital of Pennsylvania.
   - _Trenton_ is the capital of New Jersey.
   - _Dover_ is the capital of Delaware.
   - _Annapolis_ is the capital of Maryland.

3. Draw three brown triangles on the map to represent the location of each mountain range. Then label each mountain range on the map.
   - The _White Mountains_ stretch from northern New Hampshire through northern Maine.
   - The _Green Mountains_ stretch across central Vermont.
   - The _Adirondack Mountains_ are found in northern New York.

4. Color or trace each body of water on the map blue. Then label the river or lake.
   - Moosehead Lake is in central _Maine_.
   - Lake Champlain forms the border between _New York_ and _Vermont_.
   - The Long Island Sound is south of _Connecticut_.
   - Cape Cod extends from the southeastern part of _Massachusetts_ into the Atlantic Ocean.
   - The source of the Susquehanna River is in _New York_. It flows through Pennsylvania and Maryland.
   - The source of the Delaware River is in _New York_. It forms the borders between _New York_ and Pennsylvania and between Pennsylvania and New Jersey.
   - Niagara Falls is part of the Niagara River, which forms the border between part of _New York_ and Canada. Label Niagara Falls.
   - Delaware Bay is east of _Delaware_.
   - Chesapeake Bay divides most of _Maryland_ into two parts.

Page 32
Use the map below to check the appropriate parts of problems 1–5.
(Map shows approximate locations.)

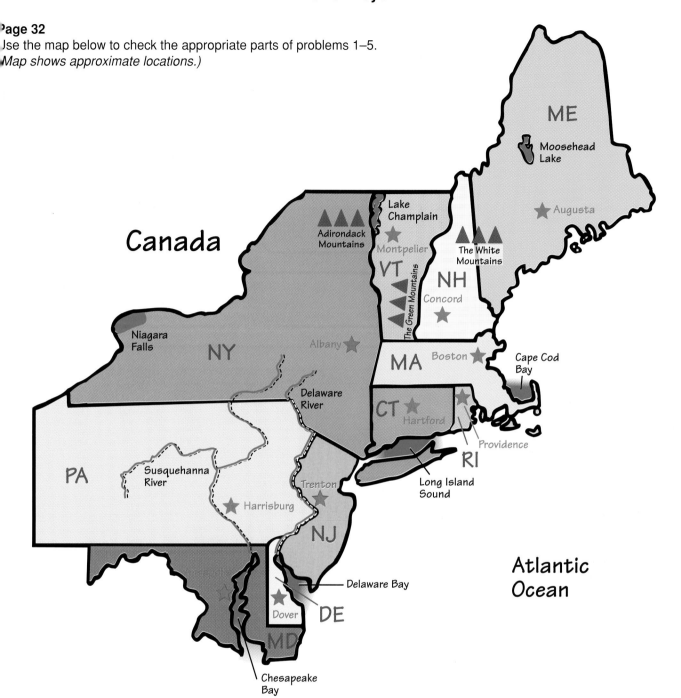

Activity Checklist

Northeast	Solved the Mystery State pp. 8–18	The "Maine" Facts pp. 20–22	Portland or Bust! pp. 23–24	Guess Who pp. 25–27	The Lobster Company pp. 28–30	Beyond the Borders of Maine pp. 31–32	Pick-a-Project pp. 34–36	Pick-a-Project Contract pp. 34–36	Pick-a-Project Rubric pp. 34–36
Student Names									